294.3
S
C 1

SERAGE, NANCY

THE PRINCE WHO
GAVE UP A THRONE
TORY OF THE

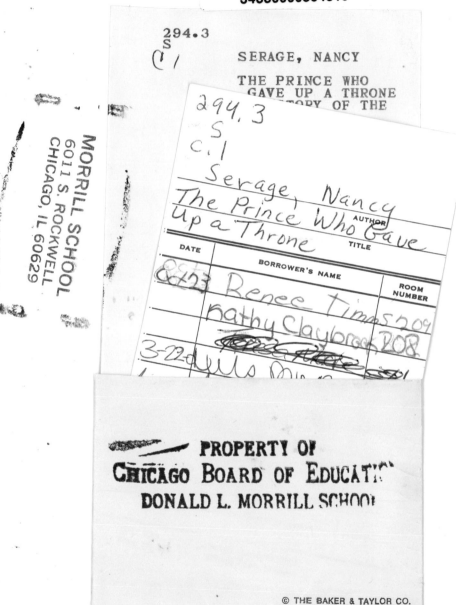

294.3
S
c.1
Serage, Nancy
The Prince Who Gave
Up a Throne

AUTHOR

TITLE

DATE	BORROWER'S NAME	ROOM NUMBER
8-23	Renee Timms	209
	Kathy Claybrook	208
3-22		

THE PRINCE
WHO GAVE UP
A THRONE
❁ *A Story of the Buddha* ❁

THE PRINCE
WHO GAVE UP
A THRONE

❁ *A Story of the Buddha* ❁

BY NANCY SERAGE

Illustrated by Kazue Mizumura

Thomas Y. Crowell Company
New York

This book is dedicated to my Guru.

THE PRINCE
WHO GAVE UP
A THRONE
❁ *A Story of the Buddha* ❁

❁ *Chapter 1* ❁

Long ago in the kingdom of Kapilavastu, on the border between Nepal and India, there ruled a king and a queen. The king's name was Shuddhodana and the queen's name was Maya. They were good, kind rulers who loved God and worshiped Him as all the people in their country did. Each day they went to the temple with gifts of gold coins and sweet fruits. The king and queen prayed to God, and they bathed in the holy water of the temple to make their bodies clean and pure.

Although they loved God very much, there was one prayer dear to their hearts that He had not yet answered. No prince had been born to these royal rulers, no prince who could inherit the throne. They dearly wanted a son who would be a great king like his father. This was the prayer that had not yet been fulfilled.

Kapila was the capital city of the kingdom of Kapilavastu. Within the high walls that protected the city from unfriendly visitors, there were many houses. The poor people lived in the smallest houses made of mud. These were hidden behind bigger houses of wood and plaster, painted pink or blue or yellow, where the middle-class people lived. Above all of these houses rose the towers of the palaces belonging to the king and all his family. Some of the palaces were made of marble, and some were made of stone covered with gold and silver. They were so bright that they sparkled in the sunshine and gleamed in the moonlight.

Within the palaces were many gardens. Each chamber had doors and windows that opened into a courtyard. Water softly splashed in fountains, and beds of sweet-smelling flowers filled the air with fragrance.

The palaces had high walls around them so that the people inside could not look out into the city and the people in the city could not see into the palaces.

The king and his family, his friends, his servants, and all the government officials were comfortable and happy at every season of the year. They were cool in the hot season and dry in the rainy season. When the winds blew dust all over the land in the dry season, they were sheltered by the carefully watered trees in the palace gardens.

The other people in the kingdom led a very different life. They were not so comfortable and content as those within the palaces. The farmers worked hard outside the city walls of Kapila while the oxen worked hard for the farmers. Inside the city the metalsmiths, ivory carvers, leather craftsmen, and artists busily made fine goods for the king and queen and for the merchants, who sold these wares in the street markets. Women wove silks and cottons, dyeing the materials brilliant colors—red, orange, purple, yellow, green, and blue.

3

The most exciting times of the year for the people of Kapilavastu were the religious holidays. On such days they enjoyed music, dancing, and games. Usually there was a procession in which elephants pulled an enormous cart through the streets. The cart was made of wood and carried a tall tower painted in bright colors like the temple tower. Within the cart was a statue of God as the people imagined Him to be, and they bowed down in worship as it passed.

Queen Maya went often in the evenings to the temple, where she would pray in the hall of a thousand columns and bathe in the lotus tank of holy water. Then she would return to her palace, to her white marble chamber, and go to bed. A refreshing breeze would stir the red flowers outside her window, and the sound of the fountain splashing would soon put her to sleep.

One evening after her trip to the temple, the queen dreamed a strange dream. She dreamed that a great white elephant, with six tusks decorated with bands

of gold, came down out of the sky. As he approached her, he became smaller and smaller until he was tiny. Then he disappeared into her right side.

When morning came, Queen Maya remembered this strange dream quite clearly, and she hurried to tell it to the king. The king was very much puzzled when he tried to think what it could mean; so he called together eight wise old men who lived in the city and asked them to interpret the dream. These eight wise men were astrologers, who foretold events by means of the stars. They listened to the king, and thought and talked together, and then they said:

"According to the position of the stars last night, O king, we believe that Queen Maya will give birth to a son. In time he will become a great leader of men."

When the king and queen heard these words, they rejoiced. God had answered their prayers. They would have a son to be heir to the throne.

Months passed, and the time approached for the birth of the baby. One hot morning the queen decided to spend the day in a cool and quiet garden not far from the city of Kapila. A procession was arranged with guards and the queen's serving ladies to accompany her. The queen was carried in a litter by four strong men to the gardens of the Lumbini.

When Queen Maya stepped upon the soft grass and felt the breezes and smelled the Mandarava flowers, she was especially happy. She reached up to pull down a branch of the blossoms.

At that very moment the baby prince was born. He appeared from her right side. No mark was left to show whence he had come, and he caused his mother no pain.

The whole world seemed happy at his birth. Everywhere flowers and trees burst into bloom. Birds sang, and animals spoke to one another, rejoicing.

The baby was not like other babies. He arose immediately and took seven steps toward each of the four quarters of the world—to the north, to the south, to the east, and to the west. Then the newborn prince spoke

His eyes and hollow cheeks were bright with fever.

The prince said, "Khamda, again I see a sad sight! Tell me, what is the meaning of this? What is wrong with this man who seems to suffer before us?"

"My dear master," replied the charioteer, "this man is ill. Have you never known illness yourself? All men and all living things in this world suffer from illness. Forgive me, my lord, if I add to your unhappiness."

"Dear friend, this is indeed a day that I shall never forget. Yes, I have had small illnesses in my life. But never before have I thought that everyone and everything in the world must suffer so. It is more than I can bear. Where is there any happiness in the world?" cried the prince. "Let us return to the palace."

And Khamda again turned back the chariot, to the surprise of the people and the guards at the palace gate. Siddhartha re-entered his marble chambers.

This time he found Yasodhara there with the infant Rahula. They were playing and laughing and listening to music. One lady plucked a harp, and another played a flute while a third danced and tried to make little Rahula dance with her. Everyone was laughing, and no one noticed Siddhartha. He stayed quietly in the doorway until his sorrow became too great for the gaiety before him.

"Perhaps if I go to the forest after all, it will be peaceful there and I can think. I must find that which never grows old or changes, and that which is always healthy and never suffers. Is there such a thing in this world?" he wondered.

Siddhartha went into the courtyard and again called to Khamda.

"Let us try once more to go to the forest. There is no peace or quiet in the palace," he said.

For the third time Siddhartha and Khamda rode forth into the city. The crowd was still in a holiday mood and rejoiced at another sight of the son of their king.

Before the chariot had progressed far down the street, a third vision appeared before the prince and his

driver. It was the vision of a funeral procession. The body of the dead man was wrapped in a robe and carried in a litter, surrounded by friends and relatives who wailed and sobbed aloud.

"Dear Khamda, what is this sad sight that is now before us?" asked the prince. "Why do these people wail and groan? What is wrong with the man who is wrapped from head to toe in his robe?"

"My prince," replied the charioteer, "this is the greatest sorrow of all. This is death that is now before us. The man in the robe is dead. He will not speak nor move again, and these other people are his family and friends who have loved him. Great and deep is their sorrow. But have you never known that death is the final end of all that lives?"

"No, no," cried the prince. "Somewhere there must be something that never dies! It is this that I want to find. Until I too die, I will search for that which never changes, which never suffers but is always in joy, and which never dies. But where shall I begin my search?

Shall I return to the palace or go to the forest? Drive on, Khamda, for I know not what is best."

The charioteer drove down the road, out of the city gates, across the country to the edge of the forest. When they reached the cool shelter of the trees, Siddhartha stepped down from the chariot and entered the woods. He sank slowly to the ground, his mind heavy with thought, and he sat in absolute silence without moving.

Where shall I begin my search? he asked himself again, and he prayed as he sat in the quietness. As if in answer to his prayer, the figure of a man appeared. He wore a yellow robe and carried an empty bowl and a staff.

"Who are you?" asked the prince.

"Gentle sir," replied the stranger, "I am seeking God. It is He who is without change, who is constant joy and eternally alive. I have found His voice within myself, and so I live in the peace of the forest and do not worry about owning many things. I wander about at will. When I have need of food, I find it."

When he finished speaking these words, the stranger disappeared.

The prince thought, "This is the path for me. I have found it at last!" and he rejoiced within himself.

He rose up from under the tree, re-entered the chariot, and returned with Khamda to the palace.

❁ *Chapter 5* ❁

The great fireball of the sun was setting when Prince Siddhartha returned to Kapila. He went immediately to his father to tell him of his decision.

"Dear father, beloved monarch of this kingdom, what I must say now will distress you. I must leave Kapila. I do not want a throne, or a palace, or any of the pleasures of this life any longer. I want the joy of God that never changes. I want to find Him because I can never lose Him through death. Only He can explain away the sorrows of this world. Allow me, dear father, to become a beggar-priest and to live alone in the forest."

"Never!" cried the king. "Oh, my beloved son, what

an arrow you have shot into my heart! Love God and do your duty here. You were born to be a king."

"My duty is no longer here," answered Siddhartha sadly, and he went to his chambers.

Immediately the king ordered guards placed at the doors of the palace walls and the gates of the city.

"He shall not leave. He must not leave." The heart of the great king ached.

The prince did not tell Yasodhara of the unusual events of the day. Neither could he pretend that he had enjoyed his trip to the forest as he had expected. The change in him was great, and Yasodhara saw it and quietly wept.

Night came, and they went to their beds. The prince was surrounded by the pleasures that had always satisfied him, but now they tormented him, and he could not sleep. Soft voices were singing. The splashing fountains cooled the air of the chamber. Fragrant blossoms swayed in the moonlight outside the windows. Rahula slept. Yasodhara slept. Finally the sound of sing-

ing could no longer be heard, and the singers, too, slept.

Then the prince, strong and determined of heart, rose from his bed and dressed. He dared not look upon his family, but silently stole from his room and descended to the courtyard below. Everyone was asleep.

Siddhartha woke Khamda. "Come, my friend, for the last time prepare yourself and the good horse Kanthaka for a journey."

The word of the prince was like magic, and immediately all was ready for their departure. The palace gates and the city gates opened wide before them. The guards slept. It was as if angels lifted up the hoofs of Kanthaka. Not a sound did he make as he carried the prince and the groom through the city and the countryside, on toward the forest.

As the sun, the eye of day, arose in the east they reached the forest, and there Prince Siddhartha said farewell to his friends Khamda and Kanthaka. The good horse dropped tears and licked the prince's feet.

"Khamda," said the prince, "I cannot find proper

words to thank you for your help and loyalty to me."

Khamda knelt before his master, and he too wept. "I did not wish to bring you here," he said. "It was done somehow against my will. The king, your father, and the princess, your wife, what will they say? Surely you will not leave them all forever? Their hearts will break. Oh, do not do this thing!"

"Khamda, be comforted. We shall all be separated some day by death. I seek God. If I fail to find Him, I shall never return home. If I do find Him, then I will return and tell you and all the world how to seek Him. Take these jewels and my crown, and put them into my father's hands."

As he said this, Siddhartha removed his royal crown, necklaces, rings, and the heavy earrings which had stretched the lobes of his ears. With his sword he cut off his long, wavy hair. Then he threw the hair to one side and gave the sword to Khamda.

At this moment a stranger appeared, wearing the simple yellow robe of a monk.

The prince said to him, "Would you exchange your robe for mine? I wish to be rid of these royal garments."

The man willingly made the change and disappeared as he had come. Siddhartha wrapped himself in the yellow robe. Waving farewell to Khamda and Kanthaka, he entered the forest.

Slowly, with dragging feet, the horse and the groom started on the journey homeward. Kanthaka would not touch food or water all the way. Though it had taken only one night to travel the road with the prince, without him it took eight days for the horse and groom to retrace their steps, so slowly did they move in their sorrow.

Great were the unhappiness and confusion and uproar in Kapila when Khamda and Kanthaka returned without the prince. The heart of Yasodhara broke, and she said to the groom and horse, "How could you take my lord away from me? Oh, Khamda and Kanthaka! You knew the orders of the king and yet you disobeyed."

"Princess, it was against my will that I bore your master forth to the woods. A greater will than mine was guiding me. It was the fate of this noble prince. Forgive us, princess."

The king was in the temple praying when he learned that the horse and groom had returned without his son. He cried out, "Thus it was prophesied by Ashita!" and he fell to the floor, heavy with sorrow.

❖ *Chapter 6* ❖

As Prince Siddhartha entered the stillness of the forest, deer and peacocks came forth as if to meet him. Before the prince had gone far, he came to a hermitage, a group of simple wood-and-mud shelters, where many monks lived and worshiped. The monks rose from their places under the trees where they had been praying and came forward to greet the prince.

"We know of you," they said, "and we consider it most remarkable that such a young man should give up a great kingdom to seek God."

"Dear friends," the prince replied, "this is the first hermitage that I have visited. Kindly explain to me your way of life. Perhaps this will be the path for me to follow."

"Gladly," said the hermits, and they led him to their temple. Within it he saw a large and beautiful statue on an altar. The statue was dressed in gorgeous silk bordered with gold. Its neck, arms, and ankles were hung with jewels. Flowers formed a crown for its head, and fruits, sweetmeats, and rice were heaped at its feet.

"Our lives are given to serving the form of God that we see in this beautiful statue," the hermits explained. "We care for His comfort and honor Him in every way we know how—for the Lord is within this statue as in all that He has created."

When the monks had finished their explanations, the prince felt within his heart, "Surely there is a better way than this. If God is in all that He has created, then He is in all men and within me. It would be better if we spent our time serving God in one another. And better yet to find Him within ourselves and offer all our thoughts to Him in the temple within."

So the prince politely thanked the monks, who had tried to help him, and prepared to leave.

"Do not go until you have shared a meal with us in friendship," they said. "We have enjoyed your presence and will be sorry to see you go."

After a lunch of berries, nuts, and rice, Siddhartha said farewell, and the monks gave him directions for finding other hermitages where the way of life might satisfy his searching.

For months the prince journeyed through the great forest, visiting one hermitage after another, but never finding a teacher who could give him the help that he needed. Finally he came to a quiet opening beside the Neiranjana River, and decided that he would stay there. He built a shelter of tree branches and reeds from the river. This protected him from the sun and rain. He found that there were fruits and nuts growing nearby in the forest. Since he had lived a life of luxury for so long, he tried now to eat little and to live as simply as possible.

Five wandering priests came to stay with Siddhartha. They recognized that his heart was pure and strong in the desire to seek God, and they hoped that he could show them the way.

For nearly six years Siddhartha and his five disciples lived in the forest. They almost starved themselves, hoping that God would answer their prayers if they denied themselves all comforts.

Then one day a thought came to the prince: "This is not the true way. I cannot think about God when I am suffering from hunger. I will eat properly and satisfy the needs of my body, and then I will continue praying."

Thinking thus, Siddhartha went to bathe in the river to make his body comfortable, but he was so weak that he could hardly climb the river bank. The trees on either side bent down their branches like arms to support him.

From a spot nearby the daughter of a cowherd saw the weakness of the prince. She filled a bowl with cow's milk and brought it to him.

The five companions of the prince, seeing that he

drank the milk, believed that he had given up his desire for God. So they left him by the Neiranjana River.

All alone but strengthened by the fresh milk, the prince seated himself beneath a bo tree in a position that quiets the body. With legs crossed and each foot upon the thigh of the opposite leg, he placed his hands in his lap. With his eyes partly closed, he turned his attention to a starlike light in the inner darkness of his forehead.

In a voice of determination he announced, "I will not rise from this place until I have heard the Word of God."

Now the devil, whose name was Mara, heard these words and trembled with fear and anger. He thought: "If God does reveal Himself and His Word to this determined prince, then the prince will announce God's Law to all the world. The whole world then will turn from evil to good and my power on earth will be destroyed. I must distract this youth from his concentration on God."

❁ Chapter 7 ❁

Mara took up his bow and his arrows of evil. They looked like lovely toys made of flowers. However, they deceived people who sought only pleasure, for these arrows caused great pain.

Mara stood before the prince and said, "Come, Siddhartha, leave your seat and join me in some sport. I have heard that you are the greatest archer in the world. Show me. Here. You may use my flower-wrought bow and arrows."

The prince did not answer the devil. He did not move, nor did he even seem to notice Mara's presence. In great anger, Mara roared in a thunderous voice, "If you will not use my bow, then I will do so myself."

With that he aimed a poisonous arrow at the prince.

Still Siddhartha paid no attention to the devil. The good thoughts in his mind seemed to protect him, for the poisonous arrow fell harmlessly to the earth.

Then Mara, in a fury, cried, "Ho, my demon warriors, come! Come from every corner of the world! Bring your weapons, and help me to conquer this determined prince!"

From the river, from the trees, from the earth and air, a monstrous horde appeared. There were enormous demons, and there were tiny ones. Their bodies were of many colors—purple and yellow or half-red with splotches of green. Some had buffalo heads with elephant trunks. There were others with anteater faces and swordfish jaws and spines the length of their skinny bodies. There were some that did not have shapes at all, but moved like masses of jellyfish. They emitted every kind of sound, from a squeal or a grunt to a roar.

When the demons had all gathered in a great circle around the bo tree, Mara shrieked, "Attack!"

Siddhartha ignored the monsters that surrounded him. When one demon caused a shower of stones to rain out of the sky, they turned to flowers that fell gently on the prince. Another demon threw a mountain into the air, but it was shattered into thousands of harmless pieces. Swords could not touch the prince, but were turned aside as if by an invisible hand. Arrows, rocks, lightning, and fire were all turned back upon the demons who threw them. They howled all the louder and ran and flew, anxious to escape from the prince under the bo tree.

At last the attack was over. The demons returned to their homes throughout all the earth, and Mara crept away defeated. He dared not even look back at the prince who had so mysteriously resisted evil.

Siddhartha was thankful that temptation was gone at last, and he continued his meditation upon God.

As the night slowly passed, he went deeper and deeper into his meditation. He felt as if he were floating in space. A peace and joy greater than any he had ever known or imagined filled his whole being. He seemed to be everywhere in space at one time, and he could see the lives of people all over the world and feel their suffering and know their thoughts. Higher and higher he rose, and then he was embraced by an ocean of light. Waves and sheets of light surrounded him. He heard the music of the spheres, of harps and bells and cymbals. And love vibrated through all the light and sound, and folded him close.

Into the mind of the prince there flooded the knowledge of God's Law. God placed in his consciousness eight commandments to give to all people. Siddhartha had become a Buddha, an Enlightened One.

When morning came, the Buddha arose from under the bo tree. He wished to begin immediately on the work that was his to do, and he decided that he would go first to the Deer Park in Benares, where other holy men before him had gathered.

The five disciples who had deserted the Buddha the day before were praying in the Deer Park when he

approached. From a distance they saw him coming and they said to one another, "Here comes Siddhartha, who has become weak in his resolution to seek God. He is probably looking for food. Let us ignore him."

But even as they finished speaking, they were impelled by the magnetism of his goodness to rise and go to meet the Buddha and to bow down before him. "Accept us once again as your disciples," they pleaded.

The Buddha touched each man on the head and welcomed him as a follower. "To you will I first preach the Law as I have learned it," he said. "It is known as the Eightfold Path. Follow this path as long as you live, for it is the Way to Heaven.

"First, you must have right views. This means that you must seek to know the truth about this world and God.

"Second, you must have right aims. These are to serve God in every thought and word and deed.

"Third, you must have right speech. You must say only that which is true and kind.

"Fourth, you must have right conduct. Right conduct is that which gives true happiness to yourself and to others.

"Fifth, you must have right occupation. Find the work for which God intended you. Right occupation will never cause harm to another living being.

"Sixth, you must exert right effort or self-control. This is necessary for you to overcome bad habits and to become perfect.

"Seventh, you must employ right thinking. Thoughts that are constructive and kind lead to happiness.

"Eighth, and last, you must practice right concentration, which is meditation upon God.

"This is the Law. Live by the Law and you will attain to Heaven."

When he had finished this his first sermon, the Buddha resolved to return to Kapila as he had promised. He journeyed for almost a year before he came once again to the gates of the city. Many times he stopped to preach to the people, who saw his calm and radiant face and asked him to share his holy knowledge with them. Many of the people became his followers and joined the five disciples.

When at last the Buddha approached Kapila, he was followed by a great throng. Word had reached King Shuddhodana of the coming of his son, and he sent forth a messenger to greet him.

The messenger came before the Buddha and said, "Lord Buddha, I bring you the love and greetings of your father the king and of all your family. The entire city rejoices at your return. King Shuddhodana and Princess Yasodhara invite you to stay in the palace. They pray that you will enlighten them on the Law which has been revealed to you."

The Buddha accepted the invitation, and with his followers entered Kapila. If the joy of the people had been great when first they saw their prince six years before, their gladness and respect were even deeper now on seeing the Buddha.

When the father and son met again after the six

years, King Shuddhodana bowed before the Buddha, who no longer seemed like an earthly being so great was the aura of goodness and purity that surrounded him. Neither could Yasodhara meet the Buddha as her husband. Instead, she knelt before him and asked him to be her teacher.

At first the family was sorry to realize that the prince was no longer the same, but when he taught them the truths that he had learned, they thanked God for sending the Buddha to them as a teacher.

After spending many days preaching in the palace to the multitudes in the city, the Buddha departed with his followers. First he led them to the north, where he had not yet preached the Law. Then he led them to the east and west, until everywhere in the land the people had heard the Word of God.

Years and years passed, and the Buddha continued to walk throughout the land, wearing a yellow robe and carrying his monk's staff and his begging bowl in his hand. Many of his disciples stayed with him, seeking to become perfect according to his teachings. The greatest of all of these followers was Ananda. He earned the special love of the Buddha by his perfect trust in him, and by his devoted and willing obedience to all the commands of the Buddha.

Never did the teacher and his followers go hungry, nor did they lack a bed and shelter at night. Wherever they went, people were happy to share their food with the holy men and to give them cots and bedding on which they could rest comfortably. Never did the Buddha doubt that God would give them all that they needed, and never did He fail them.

When he was eighty years old, the Buddha was resting one day with his disciples on the banks of the Neiranjana River. The teacher spoke to his dearest friend and disciple Ananda:

"Dear Ananda, my life span is almost over. Soon I will leave my body. When I am gone, do not let the brothers feel sorrow. They must not think that their teacher has gone because I have gone. God is their

teacher. His Law that I have given to you will lead you always like a lamp in the darkness."

Ananda, when he heard these words, wept.

"Do not weep, dear friend. It must be so in this world. Only God does not change. He will not forsake you. Seek Him by living the Law," said the Buddha, as he tried to comfort his friend.

Then the devil, Mara, appeared before the Buddha as he had appeared years ago before the moment of the enlightenment. Still hoping to stop the spread of the Law which threatened his kingdom on earth, he said to the teacher:

"Die now, Lord Buddha. Why stay on earth any longer when you may be sure of the delights of heaven? Do not the angels call your name?"

And the Buddha answered, "Peace, Mara. Your concern does not come from kindness of heart. But you will not have long to wait before your wish will be fulfilled. I die soon."

✿ *Chapter 8* ✿

Evening approached, and the Buddha rose and with all his followers proceeded to the nearby town of Vesali to ask for alms.

Kunda, a worker in metals, heard of the approach of the holy men. He hoped to be of service to them, and he prepared a great dinner of dried boar's flesh, rice, and sweetmeats. Then he went out to meet the Buddha to invite him to share the food. Thankfully, the teacher and his disciples went to the home of Kunda.

As the food was about to be served, the knowledge entered the mind of the Buddha that the boar's flesh was no longer good but poisonous. He knew that his body must have a reason to die, but that it was not time for the others to suffer. He spoke to Kunda:

"Friend, I alone will eat the flesh of the boar tonight. Would you serve the brothers with the rice and sweet-meats?" And Kunda, without suspecting the reason for the request, did as he was asked to do. When the Buddha had eaten some of the meat, he became ill, and strong pains shot through his body, but he controlled himself and appeared as if well.

After the dinner the disciples bathed in the river, and feeling refreshed, they gathered around their teacher on the riverbank. Then the Buddha spoke: "Dear Ananda, bring me a cover and place it on the ground. I am weary and must lie down."

When the friend had done as he was asked, the Buddha lay down on his side and continued: "Now, Ananda, you must go into the village and announce to all the people that this night the Buddha will leave his body, and his body will die."

Ananda wept again. His sorrow could not be eased,

but he did as he was told and went to the village and announced to all the people that the Buddha, the Enlightened One, would pass out of existence that night.

The men and women of the village wept and wailed, even as Ananda and all the disciples wept. When Ananda returned to the place where the Buddha was lying, he saw that the trees which sheltered him had burst into bloom, and the flower petals were falling and drifting down, caressing the body of the Buddha.

"Dear Ananda and beloved brothers, I take farewell of you. Keep the truth before you as a lamp in the darkness. Try, try, for as long as existence lasts, and peace will come."

These were the last words of the Buddha, and as his soul left his body, the earth trembled and shuddered in sorrow.

❀ *Author's Note* ❀

In the nine years that I taught art appreciation at the Cleveland Museum of Art, I told the story of the Buddha many more than a hundred times to children of all ages. Almost always I made it a part of a general tour of the museum collection, as well as including it in the lessons on India, China, and Japan.

If I made the story interesting to many people, this was because I loved it. The story never ceases to inspire me because it is about a man who had such complete faith in God that he could leave behind all the glory and comfort of the known for the unknown beyond mind and sensation. Because his purpose, attention, and devotion were so intense, God rewarded him by freeing him from human limitations and allowing him to share in the divine joy and wisdom which is the birthright of us all.

The Buddha was born a prince of the Sakya clan of the kingdom of Kapilavastu on the southern border of Nepal. He may have been born in the year 563 B.C.; however, different dates are sometimes given. His name was Siddhartha

Gautama. He married a princess whose name was Yasodhara, and they had one son named Rahula.

Siddhartha gave up his rank and throne at the age of twenty-nine and withdrew to the forest for six years of constant meditation. The climax to his religious seeking came when he experienced a state of conscious union with the Infinite Consciousness. He was thirty-five years old at the time. From then on he was known as the Buddha, which means "the Enlightened One." The rest of his life he spent in walking throughout the country, preaching, and training disciples.

At the age of eighty the Buddha died, or passed consciously into a state of enjoying his oneness with God. After his death the disciples of the Buddha met in counsel and organized the teachings of their master into books known as the Buddhist sutras. In 259 B.C. the Indian king Asoka sent the first Buddhist missionaries to Ceylon and China. From that time on, the religion spread throughout the Far East, where it still has millions of followers.

The Buddha preached his doctrine to the people of India several centuries before Christianity came to the West. Yet the Buddha brought a similar compassionate message of salvation to all. Brahmanism, the dominating religion of his time, emphasized the performance of rituals and ceremonies to achieve salvation. Only those belonging to certain castes, or social groups, of India were taught and allowed to perform these ceremonies. Not all could hope for salvation or freedom in God. The Buddha taught instead "the Eightfold Path" for all to follow regardless of the caste to which they belonged. The eight commandments he gave are included in *The Prince Who Gave Up a Throne*.

This version of the story of the Buddha is based on the *Buddha Karita* of Asvaghosa, the Buddhist sutras, and on endless other studies. I do not believe that I have misinterpreted the experiences of this great man. However, I have changed the emphasis of the story from a desire to escape pain to a desire to find eternal joy.

My description of the city of Kapila was created out of my own memories of existing temples, palaces, and villages of India, which I visited in 1955. There is little archaeological evidence of how the Indian people lived in the sixth century before Christ.

I hope that you enjoy the story as I have enjoyed telling it.

About the Author

Nancy Serage is a native of Ohio. She attended the Ohio State University School and received her B.F.A. and also M.A. in Art Education from Ohio State. She attended Geneva University in Switzerland and the Sorbonne in Paris.

Miss Serage taught children's drawing classes and was Docent of the Cleveland Museum of Art Gallery. There she told the life story of the Buddha hundreds of times to children of all ages in her lectures on the art of India, China, and Japan. She now lives in California, where she is a renunciant in a monastic order founded by a teacher from India.

About the Illustrator

Kazue Mizumura is well known as an illustrator and jacket artist for both children's and adult books. Her busy life also includes textile designing, advertising layout, and Japanese brush drawing.

Miss Mizumura was born in Kamakura, Japan. She studied at the Women's Art Institute in Tokyo, as well as at Pratt Institute in Brooklyn, New York. She lives in Stamford, Connecticut.